FOR MARJORIE COTTON

ISBN: 0-03-086748-7 (Trade)
ISBN: 0-03-086749-5 (HLE)
Library of Congress Catalog Card Number: 79-155869
Printed in the United States of America / First American Edition

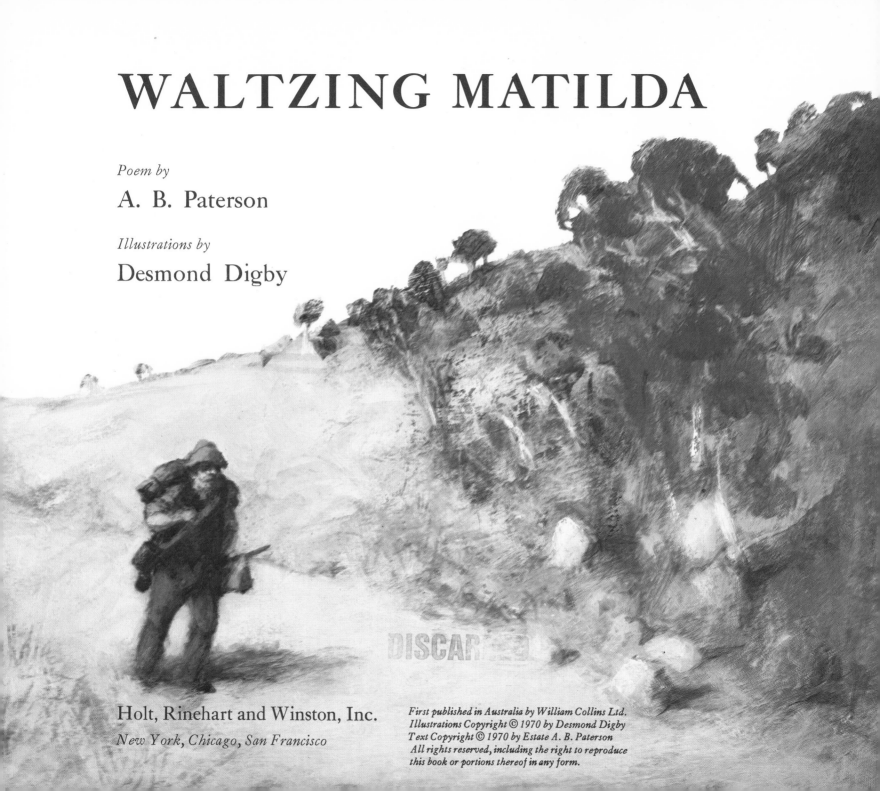

WALTZING MATILDA

Poem by

A. B. Paterson

Illustrations by

Desmond Digby

Holt, Rinehart and Winston, Inc.

New York, Chicago, San Francisco

First published in Australia by William Collins Ltd.
Illustrations Copyright © 1970 by Desmond Digby
Text Copyright © 1970 by Estate A. B. Paterson

Oh! There once was a swagman camped in a Billabong,

J 821
Pat
5.95
73-163
3-20-73
The Bright School
Chattanooga, Tennessee

Under the shade of a Coolabah tree;

And he sang as he looked at his old billy boiling,

"Who'll come a-waltzing Matilda with me?"

Who'll come a-waltzing Matilda, my darling,

Who'll come a-waltzing Matilda with me?

Waltzing Matilda and leading a water-bag—

Who'll come a-waltzing Matilda with me?

Down came a jumbuck to drink at the water-hole,

Up jumped the swagman and grabbed him in glee;

And he sang as he stowed him away in his tucker-bag,

"You'll come a-waltzing Matilda with me!"

Who'll come a-waltzing Matilda, my darling,
Who'll come a-waltzing Matilda with me?
Waltzing Matilda and leading a water-bag—
Who'll come a-waltzing Matilda with me?

Down came the Squatter a-riding his thoroughbred;

Down came Policemen—one,

two

and three.

"Whose is the jumbuck you've got in your tucker-bag?

You'll come a-waltzing Matilda with me."

Who'll come a-waltzing Matilda, my darling,
Who'll come a-waltzing Matilda with me?
Waltzing Matilda and leading a water-bag—
Who'll come a-waltzing Matilda with me?

But the swagman, he up and he jumped in the water-hole,

Drowning himself by the Coolabah tree;

And his ghost may be heard as it sings in the billabong,

"Who'll come a-waltzing Matilda with me?"

GLOSSARY

BILLABONG: A backwater from an inland river, sometimes returning to it and sometimes ending in sand. Except in floodtimes it is usually a dried-up channel containing a series of pools or waterholes.

BILLY: A cylindrical tin pot with a lid and a wire handle used as a bushman's kettle.

COOLABAH TREE: A species of *Eucalyptus, E. microtheca*, common in the Australian inland where it grows along watercourses.

JUMBUCK: A sheep. From an aboriginal word, the original meaning of which is obscure.

SQUATTER: Originally applied to a person who placed himself on public land without a license, it was extended to describe one who rented large tracts of Crown (state-owned) land for grazing and later to one who owned his sheep run.

SWAGMAN: A man who, carrying his personal possessions in a bundle or SWAG, travels on foot in the country in search of casual or seasonal employment. A tramp.

TUCKER-BAG: A bag used to carry food, especially by people traveling in the bush.

WALTZING MATILDA: Carrying a swag; possibly a corruption of "walking Matilda." "Matilda" was a type of swag where the clothes and personal belongings were wrapped in a blanket roll and tied toward each end like a party cracker. The roll was carried around the neck with the loose ends falling down each side in front, one end clasped by the arm.

ABOUT THE AUTHOR

A. B. PATERSON was born at Narrambla, New South Wales, Australia, in 1864. He became a lawyer and was still practicing when he began to write ballads that were published in the Sydney *Bulletin.* He wrote "Waltzing Matilda," which was to become practically an Australian national anthem, to the tune of an old English marching song. Paterson later became a journalist and also wrote two novels and a book of verse for children. Several collections of his verse were successfully published in Australia. He died in Sydney in 1941.

ABOUT THE ARTIST

DESMOND DIGBY is a satirical painter and theatrical designer under contract to the Australian Opera Company. Of his illustrations for children's books he says, "I think of each page as a little set. I like miniatures, probably because of my theatrical work where I do strips and strips of sketches and choose the ones to be blown up later. I did some drawings for *Waltzing Matilda* and I didn't like them, so I tore them up. I work like that all the time —it has to be right for me, I'm afraid."

Waltzing Matilda is the second book which Mr. Digby has illustrated for children. He makes his home in Sydney.